How to Change the Way You...

Your Journey to Finding Happiness

To Nerd,

you can be anything you want.
Be happy. I hope you are,
and always will be.

Love always,

Dork.

Acknowledgements

I once heard Jim Rohn say that when you pass away, all the knowledge that you have spent your whole life gathering, experiencing, and learning from goes with you. If you write down what you know, you share it with others and hopefully it does not go away. This is what I'm doing with you now.

I have chosen to undergo a conscious changing of who I am as a person, and the way I live my life. This has taken all of my adult life up to this point – I'm now age 40 – and I expect to continue to grow every day until my physical life comes to an end, a long time from now.

I will share with you what I know today that has really worked for me in creating the happy, loving and prosperous life that I have now. In subsequent writings, I hope to share with you more nuggets of wisdom that I discover from others and through self-discovery.

The self-discovery that I have been through has helped me to self-create the thoughts and beliefs that I hold today. Many ideas in life come from other sources, and as I have internalized these ideas, I spent much time honing them to make them my own. I encourage you to do the same – take this information and use what resonates with you as you read it. Internalize it and make it work for you. For all those who have inspired me, I offer a thank you for enhancing my life, as well as to the universal forces that aid me on my journey every day.

Thank you to those who have shared with me and helped me on my journey:

To my husband, Jim, who is the main inspiration in my life. To my children, Alex and Jaimie, who bring me joy every day.

To those authors and motivational speakers that have helped me to gain much wisdom over the years: Jerry and Ester Hicks, Louise Hay, Edgar Cayce, Robert Monroe, Jack Canfield, Rhonda Byrne, Michael Newton, Mary Summer Rain, Paul Pearsall, Norman Vincent Peale, Jim Rohn, Zig Ziglar, Anthony Robbins, Napolean Hill, Sheila Gillette.

Chapter One

Ask Yourself: How Did I Get to This Point in My Life?

Do you find that you think about money a lot? So much of what happens in our lives has money attached to it – you need money to live, and you live to make money for what may be many hours of your day.

Do you have a life where your job is a major part of your day? For many of us, that is what a good majority of our day consists of – getting up to go to work and spending the day there. After your long day there, you head home and get a bite to eat. Maybe you watch a show, check your email, or visit with a friend for an hour or two. Then it's time to go to bed so that you can get up early to go to work. Is that your routine?

Whether it is your routine or not – ask yourself this question – Do you love what you do for a living and the way that you live? I talk with clients everyday who tell me that they love their job and enjoy coming to it every day. It is very liberating when you don't really feel like you're working as you go about your day because you love doing those activities anyway.

So the magic question is – would you do it for free? Would you be willing to work for free because you love what you do? If you are not willing to work for free, or cannot work for free because you need the money, then you are working because you have to. You need the money to cover everything in life that you need it to cover.

Saying, "This is the job that I've chosen to do to earn my living because I want to be enjoying my life while I have this obligatory task of earning money," is a good thing.

But what if you're not doing what you love? What if you cannot say this about what you do for a living? What if you dread going to work everyday, yet you do it with commitment so that you can have your needs provided for? What if you are not doing it with commitment and you change jobs often because you think the next will be better somehow. If you do not love what you do – then you have a real problem, a problem that I am happy to say you can solve.

The nature of the problem is that it begins with a "double negative." You not only dislike your job, but now you have a negative feeling surrounding the money that comes from the job.

This creates a relationship with money that has you saying, "I don't like my job and it's all your (the money's) fault that I even have to do it. If it weren't for you, I would be free of this hassle in my life.

You will need to change both of these negatives to get to a positive. (Just like in math class – however this is an actual practical application!)

Loving what you do for a living can be liberating. It eliminates a great many problems, and changes your life in a dramatically positive way.

For example, you don't like your job so it puts you in a bad mood, and as we said before, you have a negative relationship with money because of this. The bad mood you're in flows over to affect your relationships with family and friends. Since you're in a bad mood, it seems as if more things keep happening to lock you into this feeling. The negativity is drawing you in.

Mysterious things happen to you out of the blue that are inexplicable and confusing. It doesn't appear to be happening to anyone else – why you?

Think about it. The problem is how you are thinking.

Achieving your life's goals is about giving yourself what you want in life on a daily basis. The more that you create, with your thoughts, all these good things that are just right for you, the more you will start enjoying life and the more life will begin shining upon you exactly what it is that you desire.

So maybe you're thinking something like, "Yeah, I want a million dollars, and have wanted to be a millionaire for my whole life, but there isn't a million dollars sitting in my bank account right now – so it can't be that simple!"

It is simple – it just involves a change in the way that you think. Change is one of those things that happens often in life, and yet it can be very hard to accept.

Embracing change that will bring you a better life seems like a no-brainer. Why should it be so hard to just wake up one day and say–"Okay, I'm going to start doing the things that I want to each day – things that make me happy – and more of those happy things will come my way."?

It can be that easy, but then life gets in the way – just like it has for as long as you can remember.

When you start thinking about the details of your life – whether it's the money, or the job, or the kids and their endless activities, or your health, or your weight, or your spouse, or your barking dog, or the lack of time you have and all the rushing around that you do, or it's cold and raining outside and you have to drive in it with a traffic jam to boot, or, or, or, or_____, _____, and _____(fill in the blanks). There are so many blanks to fill, that making life what you want it to be can seem very overwhelming.

Keeping your resolve to be happy is challenging if it means still grinding daily through the tasks that bog you down. You know that they are keeping you from being happy. You definitely would be happy if you didn't have to do those things.

This is where I can be of some assistance, but it really does take focus to make this work. Why should you focus on this so much?

Focus because:

You want this very much.

You know that you are meant to have a better life than you are having right now.

You want permanent change for the better – something that is going to stick.

You are a good person and you deserve to have good things happen to you.

You will finally learn how to be happy, and feel joy in each and every day while living your life the way that you want to live it.

You will never get this chance again to be uniquely you in the body that you are in today, with the gift of life at this specific point in time. It is time to embrace your gift.

The first thing that I'd like to point out is what I said just a moment ago, "When you start thinking about the details of your life…" Okay, stop. The key word here is thinking – you are thinking about all of this. Your thoughts, and how you feel when you're thinking these thoughts, are what make you start to feel overwhelmed.

Is that a good thing?

No.

Are these thoughts getting you even one inch closer to achieving your happiness or your goals in life?

No.

Should you keep thinking those types of thoughts if that bad feeling keeps erupting inside of you each time they pass through your mind?

No.

Is there some requirement that you dwell on the thoughts that bog you down as much as they do?

No.

Why do you keep dwelling in your mind on things that make you <u>feel</u> bad, or sick, or angry, or overwhelmed? Why are you thinking of them over and over, day after day?

Do you think that's what reality is all about? That this is your life's truth? That this <u>is</u> what is happening to you each day and so you take what you're dealt?

These are natural reactions to my questions. It feels natural because it is what most of us have been taught from our society every day of our lives. Family, friends, teachers, commercials, ads, television programs, movies, and watching the actions of others have shown us how we should act and react.

How we should think and act has been drilled into us consciously or unconsciously since birth. Why do you think that "reality" TV is the rage? Because people love watching other people's natural way of being, and as we watch, we absorb that information and internalize it.

We are taught by society how to react to all situations. How to act, how to feel, how to "be" so that we fit in. We learn what is the appropriate behavior to obtain someone else's approval. You act and react based upon another's approval, without giving any thought to whether you agree or disagree with this action. You wear different faces and act in different ways with different people.

Is it you in there, or is it a bunch of programming that compiles what you have become? Do you leave a situation thinking "Now why did I say that?" or "I wish I would've said…" When that happens, the person you are beneath all those layers of conditioning is stepping in and asking these questions. The result is confusion and disappointment in yourself.

This "way that you are taught to be" actually begins taking up a great deal of your daily thinking time. You dwell, dwell, dwell on what just happened. Once you realize that this is the way our society has bred us to be, you may think that you cannot trust your own thoughts anymore. Do you really know who you are or have you lost yourself somewhere along the way?

Have no fear; you are going to find you again – if you want to.

Stop for a moment – think about what you think about regularly. Yes, that's right – think about what you think about. You may have trouble starting out because we naturally wander from one thought to another. There is little intentional thinking going on with a focus and purpose.

The best way to do it is to allow yourself to think freely as you normally do, then use a trigger to remind you to check in on your thoughts. For example, you are stopped at a light while driving and you're thinking about something, and then as soon as the light turns green, it triggers you to check in on your thoughts. I think you'll find that if you consciously reveal your thoughts in this way for short snippets throughout the day, you'll find that you are indeed thinking in reaction to learned behavior much of the time.

Are your thoughts regularly including judgment or criticism about yourself or another person? At what point did you learn to be critical of others so much?

Are you worrying over someone's negative reaction to something you said? How many times have you seen others upset over something that was said to them?

Are you replaying something that you heard someone say about you yesterday? How drastically is their opinion going to change your life?

Are you replaying a scene that happened months or years ago that still bothers you? Have you seen another person bothered by an event and she brings it up over and over again?

Are you thinking self-defeating thoughts ("I wish I would have said…", or "if I had just done this…then…"? Are you coming from a place of joy or a place of lack when you communicate with others?

Ask yourself probing questions about how the nature of what you are thinking came about and you will see that all of this is learned behavior. What you have learned came from impressions that were made upon you over your life. How much each of these impressions impacted you was the result of your perception about the situation or event.

You may have some denial over the fact that what you think and say is a result of this type of programming that you have experienced and internalized over the years. This is because you know that you are a unique person with your own thoughts and feelings. You are you. Or from your perspective, "I am I!"

It may occur to you that if your thoughts are nothing more than a result of prior training from others, then maybe you're not so unique, and that others have essentially molded the framework of who you are. It is true that all your experiences, including those with others, have shaped who you are. However only you have the ability to change that shape and what you convey with your mind.

You are truly unique–no two people are the same or will think or be the same in every instance. Your personality – the real you without a physical wrapper is so very unique.

You may just be holding back the real you a bit or not allowing yourself to recognize the real you in all situations because of what you think you should say, or should do – saying what you think the other person wants to hear. But the real you is what we are here to recognize, reveal and revel in. The real you experiencing the life that you really want for yourself.

Now, let's go back to your thoughts. What are you thinking about right now? Can you check in and remember any thoughts that you had earlier today?

Are you having thoughts about all the obligatory things that you need to do like that project at work, paying bills, your shopping list, picking the kids up or doing the laundry? Or are you reliving something that happened earlier in the day or week? Do you ever worry about what other people think? If yes, why do you care so much about what someone else thinks about you? What is ultimately more important to you – what they think about you or what you think about you? Do you know what you think about you?

Checking in on your thoughts will immediately reveal the feelings associated with what you are thinking. Once you start this check-in process regularly, you will be more in tune with your emotional processes. Do you see how your thoughts affect your feelings, which then affects the way that you live your life from moment to moment?

Thoughts are your creation – no one can create them for you but you. No one can take your thoughts away from you. Your thoughts determine how you feel – whether you are happy or unhappy as you think them.

No one but you knows the sum total of what goes on inside your head. No one can change the things you think about but you. Hence, no one has the power to make you feel happy or unhappy but you.

You are the owner of your thoughts and have responsibility for them. Through your thoughts you are creating your life. I think that this is worth repeating. Through your thoughts you are creating your life. If you look at your thought patterns, you may see that much of what you think can be classified as mind chatter that comes from undisciplined thinking. If you create a process of self-discipline for your thoughts, you will start to re-program your brain into focusing on positive thought patterns instead of negative patterns. Happiness, in many ways, is self-discipline in controlling the way that you predominantly think.

Your thoughts pave the way for each and every moment, and they are what have created the life that you are living today – piece by piece (or thought by thought). That may seem intimidating to you.

Maybe you never looked at it this way before, but once you know how to make it work in your favor, this knowledge will be liberating. It will be a real joy.

Chapter Two

How Do I Make It Better from This Point Forward?

So here is the second magic question – Are you living the life that you had intended for yourself?

At some point when you were little, you started having thoughts of how you wanted the future to be. As you grew, these dreams grew in detail and vividness with you.

Do you remember any of those thoughts or dreams? Could you write down one or more of your childhood fantasies right now? Try it and see what you come up with. How easy or hard this is for you depends on the depth at which you've buried the fantasies inside of you. You may really have to dig!

If you had let them go at some point, do you remember at what point that was and how long it has been since you thought about them?

A great activity that will trigger remembering is to spend some time each night before sleeping just quietly thinking about what those dreams were. Write them down as they come to you – even if it is just a word or two. This will help to trigger your memory the next time you come back to it.

Now without judging the dreams of the past, or the feelings that they conjure up, ask yourself if you still have this dream somewhere inside of you. Do you still want this to happen?

As you are going through this exercise, see if you can find the point in time when this dream stopped being so important. Is there a particular age or an event where things changed for you?

Dreams are something that you create in your mind because you want them to happen. We all want something to happen for us, no matter how small that wanting may be. It is a natural event.

If all you are doing is <u>reacting</u> to what life deals to you day in and day out, how will you make the time for your dreams to happen?

Life is not as big an enigma as you might think. All you need to do is bring <u>you</u> back to the forefront of this experience so that you won't feel lost in your quest for who you really are and what you want in life – the real you and what the real you wants to see happen in your life.

Are you just going through the motions and dealing with daily events as they come at you?

If so, you may have said that these dreams and desires didn't happen because "life got in the way".

"When life gives you lemons…make lemonade."

There are definitely ways to change these negative reactions and what's more, you can actually cause good things to happen for you.

First ask yourself – do you believe that you have no control over what happens to you in life?

Do you feel that you have no free will when something goes terribly wrong?

16

Do you think that good things that happen to you are an act of random chance and that you just got lucky? Are you waiting for the other shoe to drop when something does go right – waiting for something bad to balance it out?

Have you ever uttered the words, "I knew it was too good to be true!"?

Then for you, this is your current truth.

To change your feelings about your lack of control over what happens to you in your life, there is only one thing you need to change. It's not about changing other people, it's not about changing anything in the universe, or about your relationship with a higher power getting better, or being nicer to others, or caring about what other people think about you.

To change your life and everything that happens to you within your own personal universe – all you need to change is you.

Let me elaborate on this last statement.

If you think about it, you make hundreds of decisions each day. You are exercising your free will as a human.

During each activity that takes place during your day, you decide what to do and not to do in various circumstances. These are your reactions.

Each time you respond to a situation, every time you make a decision about something, you are creating your life in baby steps.

In just one day, you are given thousands of choices to make for everything that you do – from the mundane to the meaningful. Will you get out of bed on time or sleep in fifteen more minutes? Are you going to take that new job or will you stay with the one you're in? All of these decisions are paving the road that is your life. There are so many actions that happen daily, hence so many choices, that your life's path over many, many years becomes a complex string of all of these decisions. Look back at where you've been. Can you see where you've made bad choices?

Bad decisions can come from many sources.

They are decisions that you learned to make either by conditioning from others (i.e. how our society tells you that you should respond), or you have distorted your own pure way of looking at things and are no longer deciding from that pure and untainted view because of something that has happened in your life that made you start seeing things differently (for example, you can't feel positive about money or believe in the potential abundance of money in your life because you've been flat broke for so many years).

External influences may have contributed to your bad decisions. However, you can control which external factors will make their way into your psyche and which will not. You get to decide what becomes real for you.

For example, someone may say, "You'll never amount to anything." It is up to you to say, "No, that is not true and I don't accept that for myself." By doing this, you have kept this external influence from becoming your reality.

Only internalize information and make it real for you if you think that it is in your best interest and is going to enhance your life. You are responsible for yourself and so if you try to really love yourself and bring good things into your life, it will happen for you.

You won't dwell on people you don't like, or the job that you hate, or the fact that you don't have enough money. You will put the past in the past, and you will begin each day feeling joy for yourself and thinking of ways that you can enjoy your day. Thinking of what is going wrong for you will only put that bad feeling back inside of you, so don't think of those things.

So back to the magic question – have you been living the life that you intended for yourself?

If the answer is no, then it is a wonderful thing that you will be given thousands of opportunities each day to start changing how you decide that road of life is going to be paved for you.

You can create a better life for yourself just by focusing on you loving you. You liking who you are as a person. You focusing on only the good things that are happening for you and giving as little attention as possible to the things that make you feel bad inside when you think about them.

If you disagree with how someone else is living their life – allow them to be who they are, and think of what you can do to make you feel better. Sometimes simply allowing others to be who they are and realizing that it does not need to impact your happiness can be all that is needed here. Controlling others is not what you are here to do – remember to focus on what you do have control over: <u>you</u> and the way you feel.

If you accidentally fall back into the old pattern of reacting to life instead of actively creating what you want to have happen for you, that's okay, because you have many opportunities throughout the day to choose for yourself in an intentional way. Once you decide intentionally instead of reacting automatically, it will be like a snowball effect and will start to happen more and more. Over time, this will be your new repetitive pattern with the majority of your thoughts and decisions during the day.

All you have to do is start realizing that your thoughts and feelings associated with every event, every day, are the key and you will have made a huge leap forward in achieving the goals that you have for your life.

Changing thousands of thoughts every day to something different may seem like a lot of work.

The good news is that thoughts are magnetic in nature, and one good thought will attract more good thoughts because you are already in that good space in your mind.

Chapter Three

How Do I Put This Into a Real-Life Situation for Me?

So lets say that one of your longtime goals is to further your education so that you will qualify for the job of your dreams.

Deciding that you want to be educated is the first step. Then you can refine that initial desire by defining specifically what you want your focus or field of study to be.

See the end result in your mind, and you will achieve the end result.

The more specific that you are about what you want as the end result of this process, the better you will be able to envision this happening for you. Do not worry for a moment about how you will get to this end result or whether or not you think it is realistic. Just envision the end result in positive detail.

I say positive detail, because there can come a point where you get into so much detail that your mind may start thinking it is too big of a goal, or that you just don't see how that can happen for you. If you start feeling negative at any point in the detail, then it is time to stop going into more detail and just take it up to the point where you were still thinking positively.

Once you get to a point where you can consistently see the end result of this goal with a positive outcome, then you will begin to be excited about achieving this goal.

Once you become excited about achieving this goal, you will empower yourself to make it happen. You will find the way to make it happen.

It is a simple process. The thoughts that you have created surrounding having the goal will begin to reveal and manifest new thoughts: the step-by-step process that you will do to get you to your goal.

Back to the example – you have the goal of supplementing your education to get you to your dream job. Your thoughts are what make this goal exist.

You now understand that you've brought this idea into your life, and you've decided that you want to go for it and see if you can really make it happen for yourself. As you keep thinking about it, you will find that eventually you will get an idea that will take you partway there. This will be a new thought that has surfaced that is an action item on your part.

As you look at the idea, you may find that you doubt its validity. You might think too hard and analyze it every which way. You can't possibly see how taking one small action, which is usually what the idea consists of, will result in the attainment of your goal.

Be brave at this point. Have the bravery to take your first step toward this idea – it has presented itself, and you can see a direct connection between it and your goal.

Taking a positive action, no matter how small, will get you one step closer to that goal. It will be much more empowering than letting doubt and fear paralyze you and keep you from realizing your dream.

Sometimes it takes many small steps to get to that end result. As long as you hold that positive end result in your mind consistently, it will eventually happen for you.

But…as you continue on this journey, let's say that "stuff happens". It has not been all roses.

If you are doing this exactly the way that we have talked about, with a clear and focused intent to get to the finale, then how is it possible that things can go wrong?

Things go wrong when your thoughts allow them to go wrong.

Two main factors come into play here. It may be that you are unconsciously thinking defeating thoughts about yourself or your ability to reach the end goal. Another factor could be that you are still overcoming a lot of negative things happening in your life right now which you had set in motion long before you decided to get positive. There definitely is a momentum that is created no matter the direction you are running. You have to slow down, and stop your momentum (running) in one direction before you can begin to run in the opposite direction.

It will take time, determination and discipline to change these two factors, which really go hand in hand in the way that they work.

Some people are not willing to take on that kind of responsibility for their thoughts. Maybe they do not believe that their thoughts have that kind of power over their lives.

Let's go back to the example of furthering your education. This dream originally was a creation waiting to happen for you. Visualize it as a "ball of thought". It was an unrealized dream because you negated the possibility that it could ever happen for you. Because of this, all it could ever be was a dream waiting to happen. You didn't believe it could happen for you and so you negated it from existence.

You started reading the words in this book, or something happened that made you change your mind about living this dream. Eventually, you decided that you would like to make this goal of being specially educated for your dream job to become a reality.

You started thinking that you could achieve this goal and you were turning your feelings of inadequacy and inability around to feelings of empowerment. You said to yourself, "I can do this!"

This is a very good start to getting there. Keep thinking this and feeling good about getting there.

Repeat steps toward empowering yourself as much as possible on a daily basis to keep you inspired.

Even with this great start, more "stuff happens" and you have a couple of bad days. You are in a bad mood and can't get out of this slump. All of a sudden, you are thinking about your desire to be educated and then you start thinking about the cost to cover that education – prices have gone up over the years and you are getting sticker shock when you figure out the total bill. You continue thinking about the money and you start to realize that there are all kinds of extra expenses associated with getting this education, and that you don't have that kind of money. You are coming up with a string of self-doubting thoughts about whether you can do this. You don't like all the burden that you perceive this will put on your budget. By the time you are done with this new negative line of thinking, you don't see how it can possibly work and you're not even sure if you still want it because it's so expensive.

After you have the revelation that it won't work because of the money, you try to make yourself feel better by justifying why this dream of yours really wouldn't work anyway. You are digging for new reasons why it wouldn't work outside of just the high cost. At this point you might bring in thoughts about your kids, who need to be taken care of while you are at these classes. You don't know who would watch them at night while you go to school, so your plans to go back to school just really won't work.

Then you think about how you'll be the oldest person in your classes and how that will make you feel. You start thinking about the young students that will be taking those classes and graduating and making all the big money while you aren't, and you feel angry that they have the freedom to do this because nothing is holding them back. You feel bitter that they are taking the job that was meant for you and how they can do it and you can't.

It snowballs. There are too many reasons why it won't come together for you and now you just feel bitter about it. Maybe you are even questioning why you entertained the idea to begin with.

These are examples of negating thoughts and patterns that will keep your goal from happening – it cannot possibly work because you've come up with all sorts of reasons why it wouldn't work. Then it never happens for you because you've thought it right out of your life, and since you've justified why you cannot make it happen down to the last detail – no one can give you a hard time if the subject ever comes up. You've got your reasons and your convictions as to why it didn't work.

It is time to stop worrying about what other people think and stop coming up with "good" reasons why you can't do this. Realize that you are also justifying the happiness out of your life, and that you are giving up your dreams because of negative thinking. You are convincing yourself that this is your reality.

Your dream of having a better life is delayed until you can have a predominant focus on the positive side of the dream. This is important if you want to be successful in achieving this goal at this point in time. The physical person that is you right now in these circumstances, this place, location, and time, will not present itself in exactly the same way again. You may wait until a different point in time, in different circumstances or in a different frame of mind. That is always an option. But why delay what you really want any further? This is your chance right now, so concentrate only on those aspects of your goal that make you feel good so that you can make this happen. The rest of the story and how it all plays out will come to you as you focus on what makes you feel good about your goal.

Just remember that you need to ignore, turn your back on, and remove from your thoughts anything that has a negative connotation surrounding your goal. Let those thoughts go. You owe it to yourself to think about what you can do, and not dwell upon what you think you can't do.

Feel good about yourself for wanting this, and feel good about achieving it as you think about it happening. Think about the end result, and smile.

Chapter Four

Let's Expand

By now, you have had some time to reminisce about your dreams and goals from the past. I want you to really dig down and remember them. All of them – and don't rule anything out as "foolish."

As you recall mentally, things will start to come back for you in bits and pieces. Do you see where there may have been points in your life where things changed and circumstances seemed to prevent your goals from ever happening?

So is it too late? Now that your life is what it is today – is it too late to change your direction? You are the one who answers that question.

One of my favorite sayings is attributed to Henry Ford, "Think you can, think you can't – either way you're right."

If you think it's too late, and that you are so locked into your life that everything, every person, every detail that is in your life today is there to stay whether you want it or not – then you are right.

If you see that there is the potential to change one or many things about your life by adjusting the decisions you make every day and your choice of thoughts, then you can make it happen. It is not too late!

As you do a mental check-in on your thoughts throughout the day, you will find that there are so many negative things that you think about on a regular basis.

The first thing you need to do is stop the negative thinking as much as possible. It will take self-discipline to do this, however it is the big gold key to the door of happiness. Do whatever you can to pivot to happier thoughts when you aren't in a good frame of mind.

As I said before, these bad feelings and negative thoughts are the pavers to the road leading you away from those things that you want in life. It is a stop sign for your goals, desires, and dreams.

Trying to retrain a lifetime of negative thinking is probably one of the most challenging things that you will ever do. Having a real commitment to changing your life is what will keep you going. Making this change in segments instead of all at once can help, and there is a bit of a trick to it.

Start by spending a day or two, or more if you'd like, tuning in to what type of thinker you really are.

Do you find yourself judging people and situations a lot?

Do you look back on situations and analyze them often?

Are you critical about how things are done?

Do you try to find something wrong with how a co-worker, friend or spouse is doing things? Do you correct him often for the sake of being right? Do you feel better when you do this, or do you feel worse?

Are you belittling people or situations, always thinking that you could do better?

Do you belittle yourself a great deal or expect things to go badly for you?

If most things seem to go wrong for you and if by chance something should go right, then do you question its validity? Do you always hold your breath when good things happen, waiting for the other shoe to drop?

Do you often say things like, "it is what it is," or "Murphy's Law," or "that's just the way it goes," or "it was meant to be," or "I must not have been meant to do it"?

Are you spending most of your time talking to others about situations that happened for you or someone else that was unfair, wrong, or stupid trying to get them to agree with what you're saying? Is this the basis of most conversations that you have?

Reveal to yourself what type of thinker you are and you will learn much in these exercises.

The way you think about and treat yourself is just as important as the way you think about and treat others.

No matter where you are at on the Positive-to-Negative scale with your thoughts, you can still achieve your life's goals and make anything that you want to happen for you happen.

I'd like to do an exercise with you now that will spark inspiring thoughts and help you to create a process that will lead you to achieving your goals.

Start with a piece of paper. Spend just a few minutes on this, keeping any analysis to a minimum. Do not place judgment on your answers in any way.

Ask yourself –

What are the most important goals that I want to accomplish or start working on in the near future?

Make this list a top five. No goal is too big or too small.

Once you've listed the five most important goals in your life for right now, put a number next to each in order of priority, with the most important being number one. The goal with the highest priority is the most important goal to you, and one that you want to accomplish first.

Next to each goal, I want to you write in the margin whether you think that goal is "easy" or "hard" to obtain.

Now highlight or underline your highest-priority goal. This goal has #1 written next to it. Do a quick mental check-in of your thoughts and capture your initial feelings when seeing yourself accomplishing this goal.

Are you feeling good or bad? Optimistic or pessimistic about it? Do you think you can make this goal happen for you?

If you are feeling bad, is it because you "don't see how this will ever happen"? Or are you thinking "this would be nice but I'd never be able to do it?"

If any type of defeating thought or feeling comes along that is overwhelming, it is time to move on.

Next, I want you to review the goals that have "easy" written next to them. Of these, which do you think is the easiest to accomplish?

Again, do a mental check-in and see how you feel about your ability to make this goal happen for you.

If you cannot get past any negative feelings that these exercises are creating, then put the paper away and stop doing these exercises right now. Only work on your goals and these exercises when you feel good.

You need to be in a state of joy, and good feelings need to be a partner to the thoughts associated with your goals. When you are feeling good again, make sure that all you are thinking about is what an absolute joy it would be to accomplish your goals. See yourself making it happen.

If you are currently in this joyful state, look at the pieces of paper that have the top priority goal and the easiest goal. Start writing under the top priority goal what you see as the details that are necessary to making this goal happen. Focus on positive details and be as elaborate as possible. If you start getting to details that drag you into a negative feeling, immediately take yourself into another direction.

You may need to start out with more basic generalities related to making your goal happen before you can get into the finer points. It may take many sessions doing this exercise to open your mind to ways you can make this happen. Details will not all come at once, they will unfold over time. Be aware and alert so that you can easily identify when you are having an inspired thought.

While filling your page with the details of making your goal happen, don't get discouraged. You have been burying your true thoughts and feelings for most of your life because of how you have been trained to think and feel. Give yourself some time to bring change to your thoughts.

Once you have finished the details for the highest-priority goal, do the same with the "easiest" goal.

After you have written all the positive details that you can about achieving this second goal, I want you to look at everything you have written for both goals.

Which goal seems to be easier now? Which one would you like to start with – the easier one or the one that is top priority?

There is no right answer; it is simply the order that you choose to start. Now it is time to choose which will be your center of focus.

It is fine to hold all of your top five goals in your mind with positive thoughts surrounding them. However, focusing on just one for now will give you the training that you need to become skilled at this.

Once you have this skill, it will be up to you to decide how many goals you focus on at one time.

One point to note is that you want to devote a great amount of time and attention to the goal at hand. Placing many goals in your sights at once can dilute your efforts. This is why we are starting with one goal; however I recommend three goals as a maximum focus at one time.

If you can, set aside a certain amount of time each and every day to thinking your positive creative thoughts about this goal. Create uninterrupted thinking time about this one thing. You will find that you start looking forward to it.

When I'm making this time for myself, it either happens right at the beginning of the day while I'm still in bed, or right at the end before sleeping. For me, this is my real time alone. In my bedroom, I've hung posters that have pictures and cue words of things that I'd like to have, or attributes that I'm working towards to stimulate positive, creative thought during this time.

If this is what you really want, and you can eliminate all negative thoughts for this short period of concentration, then you will open the door for feelings of joy to surface within you every time you do this. You will feel really good.

That is the catalyst – feeling joy as you think about this goal. Why is that the catalyst? Because you have given yourself a new life experience during this time each day. You are now experiencing joy, pure joy, again. It feels good doesn't it?

When was the last time you felt like this? The good news is, you've unlocked this feeling that has been buried beneath many layers of conditioning and the real you is coming out. The real you is learning how to create in a positive way and draw your desires into focus. Yes, it is.

Each day that you have your time of concentration, allow yourself to open your mind and clear the way for thoughts to come to you. Smile to yourself.

You may have many days where no new thoughts or details come to you. This is enough when you continue to acknowledge that you want to achieve your goal and a good feeling comes over you. Don't judge it, just be happy with yourself and know that you are going to accomplish this goal.

The more that you think about the fact that something has not happened yet, the more you are bringing negativity into focus. Allow it to take its own course and good results will come to you.

As you are open to new thought and new ideas are coming, keep writing them down on your page for that goal. Once you get to a point where you think you have enough details to put an action plan into place, you will need to begin immediately to make it happen – this is when you begin the action phase.

Start making it happen now. Don't analyze it, or let fear grab hold of you, paralyzing you from acting.

Even if you don't have the whole picture in your head – if you have enough visualized that you can at least begin your first action forward, the rest will unfold for you as you go.

Remember that even during this action phase, keep an open mind to new details and be flexible while you remain focused on achieving your goal's final outcome.

If you come to a roadblock or a place where something happens that you perceive to be negative, don't let that dissuade you. This is simply old baggage that you happen to be carrying with you.

Old baggage seems to have a way of hanging around until you can let go of the past and put it out of your present thoughts. This will take mental retraining, and it will take more than one day to change your habits. If you were able to redirect all your choices in life to be something positive in one fell swoop, then you would see how fabulously these practices work because you would have results in a much faster timeframe. Without a dramatic metamorphosis like this, you will continue to see the old baggage showing up every now and again. Accept that is has happened because of old thought patterns, and then move on.

How you react when old patterns resurface, tripping you up, is going to determine how much delay and loss of focus you encounter. If you react poorly and create negative thoughts because of an incident that occurs, then you are focusing your time and energy on your current circumstances again, throwing more negative attraction out there for it to happen again. You have just regressed back to the old days when you walked away from your dreams.

Many times I have heard someone tell me that they keep seeing the same lessons appear for them over and over because they have not yet learned. This is only because they keep giving thought to something negative every time it happens which will only attract more of those same types of negative occurrences. Stop dwelling on these incidents in your mind, and you will see how quickly they disappear.

Stay committed to achieving this one goal, and ignore any negative things that you may encounter along the way, just keep taking your focus back to your goal. Say your goal over and over again to yourself if that is what you need to do to stop from getting angry or feeling depressed or upset. Just keep saying it until you have neutralized the bad feeling.

During your focus time each day – keep it light-hearted, and full of happiness. That way you'll look forward to that pure feeling of joy when you are struggling. Remember that joy you experienced the day before and bring yourself back with something that reminds you of that time. It could be through a scene that you had visualized, or a certain smell you experienced like a candle burning, or maybe you had relaxing music playing in the background.

By putting your focus on the good things, and removing your thoughts of the past, you will start to change the way you react to life. You will start to change the hundreds, if not thousands, of choices that you make every day. Positive outcomes will spill over into your other activities and won't just be associated with this goal anymore. Diseases are not the only things that can spread – so can happiness!

As you become happier, watch your whole world change around you.

I'd like to share with you the top 5 that I had created for myself many years ago. I have achieved every item on this list and my life has become meaningful, fulfilling and has magical qualities.

While I have achieved each goal on the list and have now added new goals – I always give thanks and feel deep gratitude for what I have: the wonderful people and relationships, places in the world that I have experienced, feeling good about myself and my life, and receiving all the things that I have asked for.

My gratitude keeps these good feelings going and perpetuates the flow of good things coming to me.

Amy's Top 5

- · Find the perfect life partner.
- · Live in the place that I most like to vacation in the U.S.
- · Get my master's degree.
- · Make a six-figure income.

· Have a family that is functional, happy, and that
  lives in harmony.

Chapter Five

The Meaning of Life Itself

The entire meaning for your life, your purpose, the reason why you are here, is to experience life in each and every day, every moment, every second according to how you choose to live it.

Your life is your experience. YOUR experience.

Your experiences, how you live them, and what you have become as a person are completely up to you. You pave the way for your experiences, and your ability to change what you have paved is possible through your chosen reaction to your experiences. So if you are talking about front loading – deciding ahead of time what direction you want your life to go – you can. If you are talking about after the fact – something happens that you like or dislike, whether you love it or hate it – how you react to that is your chosen reaction, so the back-end is up to you as well.

What experiences are you supposed to have? None in particular – there is not one particular moment, event or singular reason why you are really here. Think about the experiences that you have every day. Think about what has happened in your life just in the past year. Would it make sense to say that you have one singular moment in your life as your purpose when you can probably easily recall many hundreds of meaningful moments?

The culmination of all your life experiences brought together is your purpose and is not a singular event. It is your life in total.

Don't let anyone talk you into something that they think you are supposed to do. Most importantly, don't let yourself talk you into something that you think you are supposed to do. Life is about what you WANT to do, WANT to have happen, WANT to live, WANT to experience, WANT to see, touch or feel – what you WANT for you.

Has your life become an obligatory experience consisting of one thing that you are supposed to do after the other? Are you a person who often feels guilt, and that guilt is what directs your existence?

Is there time in each day that you really feel like you are in control of your own destiny, or are you dutiful to the role you've been cast into?

How much of the time in each day would you say that you are in control of your destiny?

Would you say the majority of your day goes the way you want it to?

Do you often express to others that you are having a bad day?

Do others make your decisions for you?

Or, do you spend so much of your time trying to control someone else's life that you are not in control of your own?

Changing can be as easy or difficult as you want it to be.

Let's do another check-in. Think about how you feel most of the time. Do you find yourself laughing, smiling, feeling joy or love most of the time? Or, do you find yourself complaining, criticizing, or feeling anxious and worried most of the time?

If the answer is that you feel good some of the time, but not all, then think about the parts of your day that make you feel good and see how you can expand upon what is happening for you during those times and continue that trend. Even if the activity that makes you feel good will not continue throughout the whole day, you can always come back to that place in your mind at any time and re-live the event(s). Creating better thoughts in your mind will change the way you feel in your body.

If you are feeling anxious or worried – do you have a perpetual knot in the pit of your stomach? Begin by thinking of an experience that you would like to re-live that makes you happy. Think about one now. You will see that just by changing to a different, less worrisome thought, you have also changed the way you feel, and, if only for a moment, you have eased the pain in your stomach.

If you can keep recreating these feelings, they will start to multiply on their own and the power gained from feeling better and thinking better will flow throughout the day. You will find your anxiety lessening as you develop freedom from fear. Instead of concentrating on what you are afraid of, concentrate on what you are not afraid of. What thoughts can you have and what subsequent actions can you perform that will make you feel free?

I know that you have probably heard many times that you need to delve into the heart of your problem to overcome it. Please do not do this. If you are focusing on your problems, then you do nothing more than recreate the feeling that is causing the problems over and over. How is that going to solve anything for you?

Try to distance your mind as much as possible from thoughts relating to your problems. Do whatever it takes so that negative mental images come up in your day as infrequently as possible. Make changes in your routine that will help start new positive ways of seeing things. Start new routines that are special and that you do just for yourself to make you happy and take your mind off of your problems.

It can be something as simple as buying a pack of gum at the grocery checkout. If you like chewing gum, yet you didn't buy it in the past because it was an extra that you felt you couldn't afford, look at the small cost and see how it is really worth it if it will bring you an element of joy. It is one of life's small pleasures.

Another way to feel good and start off the day right is to repeat phrases to yourself that make you feel good. A phrase or sentence repeated over and over to yourself is known as a mantra. Mantras can work to replace negative thoughts and you will consequently feel good just by saying them repeatedly. As you are thinking them or saying them, there is no room in your mind at that moment for the negative thoughts.

My personal mantras are:

"Everything always goes right for me."

"I am going to see only what I want to see."

"Every day, in every way, I'm getting better and better."

"I love me and who I am as a person."

"I am the wealthiest woman in the world."

"I love my life."

"I want to feel good."

I say these mantras to myself in the shower as I start the day. I also check in with myself throughout the day, and if I find that I'm not in a joyful state, I start repeating my mantras to get back to a good feeling.

After repeating my mantras, I often listen to music that I love, and find that it really changes my mood, no matter how I'm feeling.

Often I'll find that the exact song, with lyrics that I need to hear to make me feel better, comes on the radio at just the right moment.

Sometimes I'll get an email or a call from someone that will lift me up just when I need it.

I use whatever tools I'm given during my experiences throughout the day to turn my bad moods into good ones. I am grateful to the universe during these times for helping me to help myself.

So when things happen that are not positive experiences, I try to change negative thoughts to positive ones as quickly as possible. Having a negative interaction with another person can sometimes make it more challenging to pivot away from negative thoughts quickly.

In addition to using mantras to bring myself into a better mood, I ask myself questions like, "Is this really worth getting upset over?"

Or I imagine myself at a point in the distant future and ask, "Looking back at this moment, would I still see this as something worth getting upset over?"

Or, "That person may be infuriating, but do I want to let someone like that have control over my emotions?"

Once I am in a more neutral state, it becomes easier to pivot to happier thoughts with my mantras. I may follow these moments by simply saying, "I want to feel good." I say it to myself, in my mind, over and over.

Before long, you will be able to quickly create new thoughts that make you feel good and help you to move past the incident. For example, I often think about my husband's face and the smile on it just after he's kissed me. That always puts me in a better mood.

No matter how much you want to, DO NOT LET YOURSELF GO BACK TO NEGATIVE PAST

EVENTS IN YOUR MIND. If you do this, you will recreate the thoughts, the feelings, and all the negativity surrounding the incident. It will happen all over again for you as fresh as the first moment it occurred. You will discover aspects of the incident that you may not have acknowledged before, and this will create new negativity. This will make you even more upset as you will blow the incident out of proportion to what really happened. If you can let it go in your mind as quickly as possible, the amount of time that it envelopes you in negativity will be minimal.

The next important thing to note is: do not call your spouse, friend, sibling, or anyone else to tell them "you won't believe what just happened to me…." and then go into great detail about it. Resist the urge to talk about it.

By talking about it, you are again reliving the moment, drawing more episodes with similar outcomes to you in the future through repeated negative thinking, and potentially spreading the negativity into another's experience. If the person you are speaking with is being told something negative and internalizes what you are telling them, it can affect them negatively as well. This result is completely up to them, but why do it to begin with?

Wouldn't it be nice if you could say, "You won't believe what just happened to me…" and follow with something really great that just happened to you?

As you are checking in with yourself throughout the day and asking yourself how you are doing? Make this a habit that you continue throughout your entire life. Is it going well, and are your thoughts what you want them to be? Are you finding yourself repeating old thought patterns during your check-in, or are new patterns developing?

If those old patterns keep creeping in, then have the remedies ready to go that you know will work, and use them to make yourself feel better right away.

I've mentioned some tools that I use, and a great thing to do is write down a list of your own personal tools that you can use. These are things that will make you feel happy or help you to create a better mood, no matter how foul your mood or situation.

Some examples could be:

- Think of a person that you love deeply
- Think about how good you look in some new clothes that you bought recently
- Look out at nature and see the beauty that it presents
- Play your favorite song
- Listen to your favorite comedian
- Pull out your cell phone and look at some pictures that you took or downloaded that make you happy
- Think about something coming up that you are excited about, like a movie coming soon, or a

vacation, or a date, or a season that you're looking forward to

· Make love

· Visualize the smile of your lover

· Exercise and work off your negative energy

· Make your favorite meal

Whatever it is that will generate a good feeling – DO IT! Do it now, do it every time you check in with yourself and you are thinking or feeling something negative. Change it up to enjoy the variety and so that you don't diminish the returns by always using the same tools.

All of this is about changing your daily choices so that you can continually feel good and live a good life.

Learning how to make your choices will ultimately change the experiences that you are having and how you feel about those experiences. Make your choices, live your experiences, and enjoy the ride!

Chapter Six

Recap the Top Ten Points

Up to this point, we have covered a lot of things that you can do internally and externally to change your life. Let's sum up those activities so that you can go over this list daily to keep you on track.

Decide on the top five things that you want to have happen for you at this point. As you complete a goal, add a new one to the list.

Prioritize and mark "easy" or "hard" next to your top five.

Pick either the top priority goal or the easiest to work on first – your choice.

Set aside time every day to mentally work on your goal. You can create pictures or power words on a poster to help you visualize during this time alone. Allow feelings of joy to come over you as you see yourself accomplishing this goal. Let your inner self bring details to you as you think about this goal daily.

As details come to you – act upon them. Don't delay – the rest of your initiatives relating to this goal will come as you are living it!

Check in with yourself throughout the day, every day, to monitor what you are thinking and feeling. Try using triggers, e.g. every time you come to a stop sign or a red light while driving, you'll do a check-in.

Use the tools that you have found make you feel better (music, personal thoughts, special pictures, watching your favorite show, etc.) This will help your thoughts pivot from bad feelings to good feelings. Smile as you do this – it can greatly facilitate your mood-changing effort because when you smile, you can't help but feel better.

Create daily mantras that you can repeat to yourself to elevate your mood and to set the stage for a great day. Bobby McFerrin says it best in his mantra, "Don't Worry, Be Happy."

Understand that life is all about the experience. Enjoy life as you are working toward your goals, and decide how you will react to daily circumstances. Think good thoughts and you will feel joy!

Your purpose in life is all about the choices you make for yourself. If you don't like what you've chosen up to this point, you can change it. It is up to you!

Chapter Seven

Sharing My Beginning Experiences

I know that up to this point, we have focused on the ways to get you what you want in life. Now I'd like to share with you some of the extraordinary things that have happened to me from childhood to present day to help you see that no matter what "place" in life you are coming from – you CAN change your life to become what you want it to become.

I want my experiences to inspire you to do all of those things you've said that you always wanted to do. Even if you are at a time in your life where you think and feel that you have nothing or worse than nothing, I want you to feel that you can change your life and have everything that you want.

In this chapter, I will share with you what most people would perceive to be extraordinarily bad experiences. Looking back at all the hard times I've experienced, I can now see that many of the "bad things" that I judged so harshly at the time have actually been the catalysts for some of the best things that ever happened to me.

In many instances, if I had reserved judgment before deciding that an incident was "bad," I could have saved myself a lot of sadness, worry and heartache. I would have reacted differently and simply said to my inner self, "Please show me how to see the good in this." By wanting to see the good

51

in situations instead of dwelling on the bad, the emotional roller coaster might have been less of a ride. I would have allowed the wonderful end results to appear, experiencing less pain in the process.

My most life-changing experience happened when I was thirty years old. I was living in the greater Cleveland area, in the small town of Shalersville, and was a Financial Planner with my own practice. I had all my family in Ohio, and I lived about 10 minutes from my sister, Julie, and her three daughters.

Julie, my elder sister by one year, had become very ill in the year prior to my thirtieth birthday. In the year 2000, she slipped on a wet spot in the frozen food section of the grocery store. It was a hard fall, hitting her head resulting in a severe case of vertigo for the year that ensued. As the year progressed, she kept falling again and again because of her vertigo. A total of fifty-two falls in one year severely depressed her immune system.

She was a full-time college student, just finishing up her degree in Sociology. Even with her illness, I encouraged her to keep plugging away at her classes, and I helped her get to and from her classes in her wheelchair.

While she was attending these classes, there was an outbreak of meningitis on campus, and we did not know that she had contracted this highly contagious, deadly disease. Her condition deteriorated quickly and soon she could not even get up to go to the bathroom. I insisted that she spend time in the hospital to find out what was going on, and she finally agreed.

After a week in the hospital, the doctors had classified her as a problem patient because of her consistent bad mood, and did little to try to help her. Very few tests were run, and none were run that would have identified her condition.

A day after they told her that the few tests that they had run identified nothing wrong, Julie asked me to take her home so that she could spend time with her daughters. I agreed. Less than two days later, she was rushed in an ambulance back to the hospital, where she was pronounced dead on arrival. An autopsy identified the meningitis about a month later.

I was so sick over this that I could not eat or sleep. I knew that she was very ill, but at her young age of thirty-one, I never imagined that she would die. Especially since the doctors were insisting that they could not find anything wrong.

My stomach felt like someone had punched it and the feeling would not subside for months. I could not stop crying. I felt that life had dealt me a losing hand.

Julie and I had an extremely hard and unfulfilled childhood with two very narcissistic, angry parents who had divorced when we were little more than toddlers.

We were an afterthought for both of them and we learned from a young age to fend for ourselves or rely on each other. Verbal and physical abuse from both parents was a regular occurrence, from mom during the week, and from dad on the weekends.

Julie usually took the brunt of the physical beatings from both parents. She was older and stood up for herself instead of being a wallflower like me.

We both considered ourselves survivors of our childhood and we used to say that if we could survive that childhood, we could survive anything. She and I were close our whole lives, and while we argued like sisters as children, we were best friends as adults, talking and seeing each other daily.

She had three children at an early age, never married, and had an ability to attract men who didn't stick around. I helped her to raise her three beautiful daughters. The middle daughter had severe disabilities and didn't learn how to walk until she was ten, but we didn't care; we loved her and took care of her, ignoring the stares of the public. Julie, motivated by my career success, resolved to make something of her own life, and started college in her mid twenties. She was just finishing her degree at age thirty-one.

Her death took the wind out of my sails. I felt that we had both been wronged and that life was nothing but one cruel twist after another.

In the year after her death, I had given up on ever being happy again. I tried to tell everyone that I was fine, but I knew I didn't want to allow myself to be close to anyone for fear that this would happen again. I was devastated after losing my lifelong best friend, and didn't want to ever be in that situation again.

When Julie died, I had been married for close to five years to my first husband, Bill, and we had a four-year-old son, Alex. Two weeks after Julie's death, I asked my husband for a divorce. Life was short and I could not see myself being married to Bill for the rest of it. After talking with him, I learned that he had been feeling the same way for some time and an amicable divorce followed within months.

In the month following her death, the courts decided to take my sister's three children and split them up because they had three different fathers. The youngest, Candice, was seven and was placed with her father, who had not seen her in five years. Candice is now 18 and has been beaten and abused by her stepmother for the past 11 years while her father turned a blind eye.

The oldest, Jasmine, who was fourteen when Julie died, was placed with me initially. Jasmine tried to commit suicide the week that she was split from Candice and was in critical care at the hospital for three days. After this incident, her great-aunt (my paternal aunt) asked to take over custody because her father could not be located. I agreed to relinquish any rights to custody of Jasmine because of my depression and inability to be supportive in the way that she needed after suffering the great loss of both her mother and sisters. My aunt took custody of Jasmine and then refused to let me see or talk with her, at the direction of my father (her brother). About a year later, the courts ended up placing Jasmine with my maternal aunt when they saw that she was being kept away from her sisters and other family.

Amber, Julie's middle daughter with the severe developmental disabilities, had a father who went through the courts to legally disown her immediately upon Julie's death. He hasn't seen her since. I freed him from any monetary support or obligation, knowing that he did not want her.

I was the only adult who had experience taking care of eleven-year-old Amber, who had epilepsy and the mental capacity of an infant, so I was given the job of being her permanent custodian.

Amber had an unusual number of grand mal seizures that year with me, and I think she was emotionally distraught from losing her mother and sisters all in one summer. She cannot talk, so I could only rely on her non-verbal signals. It was very hard to witness her convulsing and turning blue during a seizure, knowing that I was helpless to do anything. We had to keep adjusting her medication to higher dosages, which seemed to put her in a dazed state.

I did the best I could taking care of Amber and my son that year, given that I was in such a distressed state. I wore the responsible adult mask while inside I felt like I was dying of sorrow.

Money to support my family was scarce since I did not work at building my practice at all that year. Since we had very little new money coming in, we lived mostly off of income from rental property that I owned.

It was the hardest time of my life, and I could not see how anything would ever get any better. One bad thing happened after another.

My father blamed me for my sister's death; he thought that I should have convinced the doctors to do more. We are still not talking, ten years later. He lived two thousand miles away and had little idea of what I went through as the primary caregiver for Julie in the year before her death.

I worked at getting her to all her doctor's appointments, obtained a walker and wheelchair for her, cleaned her house, cooked meals, took the kids to and from school and took her to and from her classes while still running a business and taking care of my husband and son. I lifted her into and out of her wheelchair in the last weeks of her life and spoke encouraging words as she crawled through the house, to the door, then into the car to get to her appointments.

To look at my life today, you would not know that the first thirty years were a living hell that got worse from childhood to adulthood.

After my sister's death, the only thing that kept me going was the fact that I had to take care of Alex and Amber. My son Alex was born when I was twenty-six, and his birth was the first major turning point in my life. He has been a source of inspiration and love since the day he was born, and I am so fortunate to have him in my life.

If it were not for his cheerful toddler face with rosy cheeks and big blue eyes, I may not have made it that first year after Julie died. He was the one string that kept me hanging on because I did not want to forsake him or let him down. Being close to him was scary because I knew that I would not make it through losing anyone else close to me, but I knew I had to be there for him. After I would put him to bed for the night, I would have a stiff drink to quiet the emotional aloneness that I felt. Sleeping was difficult, and crying myself to sleep became a nightly ritual. I didn't care about me at all.

It added to my depression knowing that I was in such bad shape for him emotionally, and I wanted to be a better mother during that year. I could not seem to shake the bad feelings that were plaguing me every day – I was not able to pull myself out of my depression enough to do so.

This is where I was at when I decided that enough was enough. I decided it was time to move. I would leave the state, and all the painful memories, behind. Everywhere I went I was reminded of Julie, and removing these constant reminders was all I could think to do to solve my problems. It did not make sense to me to stay in Ohio with all the family disputes and finger-pointing going on over my sister's death.

I did not want to be a part of the greed-filled malpractice lawsuit that certain family members saw as their entitlement. Not one of these persons, with the exception of our much younger brother, Joe, helped out my sister during her year of illness. Her kids and I were all she had during her weakest hours. I had a great deal of anger, bitterness, sadness, and depression that I wanted to walk away from.

With my divorce being finalized, I put my house up for sale and made the decision to move to Sedona, Arizona with my son Alex. My mother begged to be allowed to take care of Amber to overcome her feelings of guilt. She and Julie were on bad terms when Julie died, and now my mother wanted atonement. I knew that the long move out West would be difficult with Amber, so I agreed.

I felt better for these decisions and believed that "getting" away was not "running" away. What I was really doing was giving myself the opportunity to focus on a new, more positive life. I needed to be able to work on me, uninterrupted.

I told my ex-husband that I was moving and taking Alex with me, and though he would miss Alex terribly, he consented. Bill never wanted to be a full-time dad, and my moving away with Alex relieved him of that responsibility. Alex, the car, and our belongings were all we needed.

I had hit bottom, and this was my way of trying to pull myself out of the hole. While I had a positive outlook on having a better life in Arizona, I knew nothing about how to really change my life for the better, and I still entertained negative thoughts, believing that life had never been good for me and that's just the way it was.

As I mentioned earlier, I grew up in an angry family – both my mother and father had extreme anger issues, and they let their anger affect their perceptions and decisions.

This anger was a constant source of learning for me growing up. I learned to be very cautious of the things that I said and did as a child. With my parents divorcing when I was five, I had many years to follow that involved constant questioning from one parent about what the other parent said about them, who they were seeing, and what the other was up to. They both exhibited extreme paranoia. I grew to hate secrets because I was constantly being told things like, "Don't tell your mother…" or the same from my mother about my father.

Both parents were so self-absorbed that they behaved as if they had no children at all. Our mother was almost never home, working during the day and with her boyfriend at night, leaving my sister and me to fend for ourselves much of the time.

As latchkey kids to the extreme, we were fortunate that the house didn't burn down or that we didn't starve to death.

I attended some schools for as little as two weeks, and then we were gone. My mother could not pay the rent, and eviction was inevitable and often. Moving this frequently made friendships impossible, and made me an easy target for teasing at school.

Julie was my only friend for most of my childhood. Even so, we were often at each other's throats, which is typical of siblings who are so close in age.

Out father was a weekend dad who was always paying more attention to his girlfriend than to us. He would often tell us lies about himself, designed to keep the truth from my mother about his lifestyle or the amount of money he had. Most of his lies would not become apparent until years later. He did not trust anyone and would tell me daily, "What's the first rule of business?" My dutiful response: "Never trust anyone." This was his motto, and he was very serious about ingraining it into our heads.

I knew that I was having a rough childhood as I was growing up. All I had to do was look at the other kids at school to see that this was true. I used to look forward to the day that I would turn eighteen, just to be out of my mother's control. Father moved two thousand miles away to California with his girlfriend when I was thirteen, so he was a non-parent from that point forward. I did try living with him for a couple of summer months before entering eleventh grade, only to find out that living with my father was no better than living with my mother, and I had cut myself off from my sister. The many phone conversations I had with Julie convinced me to come right back.

I did make it to eighteen and had become very independent, self-sufficient, and ready to live my life as an adult. While I was very independent in my decision-making, I still had a very needy side.

I had some short romantic relationships as a teenager, and in each one I always knew right away if I really wanted to be with that person. If not, I ended it quickly. I did have two long-lasting relationships; one at age fourteen for two years and the other at sixteen which lasted until college. In both relationships, I knew after the first year that it would not last, because I was not really in love with either guy. I stayed because I enjoyed the stability of being with someone familiar. Something I had longed for as a child.

Sometime during college, after a number of run-ins with classmates which led to the ending of some good friendships, I began to realize that I had become as self-absorbed as my parents, and it was costing me friends. I knew that the run-ins were my fault, but I justified it by telling myself that I didn't know how to have friends because of the constant moving I did throughout my childhood.

I also gained a great deal of weight during the end of my college days, and went from being the extremely attractive blond with a great figure to being the chubby bitch. I knew that my looks would no longer get me the things that I wanted, so I decided to try to stop being conceited and overbearing. Being overweight helped a lot with removing the conceit, and the maturity I was gaining with age helped to smooth out some of my overbearing traits.

I identified my personality defects as being the cause of my problems, and was looking for solutions to find the real me that I had lost as a child. I remembered my sweet vulnerability, and caring for others. I wanted to find out how to get that part of me back. I began reading self-help books on meditation, anxiety, depression, spirituality, inspiration, healing, dreams, shamanism, Buddhism, Zen, hypnosis, the after-life, remote viewing and out-of-body experiences, feng shui, new-age and the metaphysical. I spent most of my twenties looking for answers and trying to make personal progress.

It wasn't until my sister died that I realized that my anger problem was not gone, but thriving and in full force. The way that I looked at life was distorted, and I took things that people said to me the wrong way much of the time.

The lens through which I viewed the world was so distorted that I perceived everyone else as a threat. They all had it in for me. I perceived that, for some reason, life just never really went right for me. The only thing that seemed to be on the right track was my career, and that was mainly because I had my intelligence to bank on. No matter how screwed up my personality was, I could always use my work ethic and smarts to move my career forward. I was born with my intelligence and this was something that I could not screw up.

Having put myself through college with loans and two jobs, I needed money after graduation to start paying the mounds of bills. My strong work ethic was put into practice when I got my first postgraduate job. I was never late and never missed work.

This work ethic became a great advantage. I learned that getting ahead can result from just showing up. If employers know that they can count on you to be there every day, they will be more likely to give you the good jobs, to keep you around.

By the time I was in my mid-twenties, I was in the investment industry and was making very good money as an annuity wholesaler. This job taught me a great deal about insurance and investments because I started, right off the bat, as the teacher. When you teach something, you learn it so much more thoroughly than by just being the student. Every question that could have come up in my job, did come up. I really learned a lot and decided that I liked the business of money.

I have always made a lot of money in my career, and have always been very marketable. One of the biggest problems that I had was keeping all the money that was flowing in from going out towards the next big investment deal.

I fell in love with real-estate investing, and while it had been very lucrative for me in the '90s, putting me much further ahead financially, I became so successful at it that I began to bite off more than I could chew. The outlay of money required to purchase the real estate ended up depleting most of my life's savings.

Then came a seemingly endless string of adverse developments, taking up any money that I had left.

Many times, I was forced to go to my credit cards to cover bills despite the fact that there was a great deal of money coming in.

My health began to weaken and I was afflicted daily with various health problems and severe allergies. Because of this, I was confronted with large emergency room bills year after year.

My son contracted a chronic virus, resulting in papillomas on his vocal chords that had to be surgically removed every six months for a period of seven years.

My niece Jasmine was a troubled teenager who ended up moving back in with us when she was seventeen. The years since her mother's death had been very hard on her and she moved between family members multiple times. The move from Ohio to Arizona was equally hard on her as a high-school Junior, leaving her friends behind. We spent thousands of dollars caring for her, covering legal fees, and, when she was old enough to move out, paying the rent for her apartment.

I easily found employment in financial services after moving to Tucson, Arizona. After a couple years, I decided to change companies for what appeared to be a better job. Shortly after taking the new job, I had a huge argument with my boss, another narcissistic female, and ended up quitting on the spot. I had not had a negative encounter like this in my career before and it left me in a state of depression. After this, I was driven to become self-employed which led me to starting a practice similar to the one I had left behind in Ohio. The startup costs just about left me penniless.

I did remarry about a year after my first divorce, just after moving to Arizona. I have to say that finding my current husband was the next great turning-point that happened in my life.

My husband Jim saw the problems that I was having and would say that he had never in his life seen so many negative things happen to anyone. This was saying a lot coming from Jim, who considered himself an "unlucky" person, and who, like me, had tragically lost a sibling.

It is amazing that one bad thing after another can happen to one person for years and years. These are some of the extraordinary events that happened to me, creating so much unhappiness in my life. I blamed every event on some external force. Never would I have considered that all the bad things that happened were in any way my doing.

Chapter Eight

When I Started Getting Better

It was not until I learned about the Law of Attraction from Jerry and Esther Hicks that I started understanding what I was doing wrong. This information came to me the weekend that my sister died in 2000. It was a difficult time to try and to absorb something so profound.

Even after learning and trying to live the Law of Attraction for several years, I still was not really changing the innermost thoughts that I lived my life by. Not completely anyway.

In 2001, after my sister's death and my divorce, I found my future husband Jim. Jim is and always will be the man for me. When he and I started dating, I let him know that I was not looking for a serious relationship. It had only been 8 eight months since my sister's death, and I had just received my divorce papers in the mail that week.

He let me know that he was only available for a serious relationship, and not some kind of casual type of arrangement.

This was a bit of a shock to me, and I knew that I did not want to lose Jim if he was the right person to spend the rest of my life with.

A few months before getting together with Jim, I had made a list of all the qualities I was looking for in a man. After I had finished, I had two single-spaced pages filled with what I required of my perfect man. I made a promise to myself that I would not commit to any man who did not meet all of these requirements.

I had been dating Jim for a couple of weeks when I decided to review my list of requirements. I was amazed. He possessed every single quality on that list.

Once I realized this, I became excited and let Jim know that I was willing to become serious. I was selling my house, and had just accepted an offer on it. In six weeks I would be leaving for Arizona, and so I asked Jim if he would be willing to come with me.

He let me know that he had been anticipating my invitation, and he had an enthusiastic YES answer ready for me right at that moment!

We made the long drive across the country, and spent the summer renting a condo in Sedona. Sedona is one of the most beautiful places on the planet, and every day that I lived there, I would marvel at the awesome red rock formations and feel an irrepressible sense of gratitude.

The time spent there with Jim and Alex was a healing time for me. I was finally starting to feel positive about the future, and I began seeing great possibilities for our life together.

Leaving behind our lives in Ohio and beginning a life together in Arizona was both daunting and exciting, and it strengthened the bond between us.

Six months after our first date, Jim and I were married on top of the red rocks in Sedona, at a spot known as the Kachina Mother vortex. It is one of many locations in Sedona that is believed to be a focal point of the area's energy.

Marrying Jim was one of the best decisions that I have made in my life. After ten blissful years-our relationship is stronger than ever, and it just keeps getting better.

One great thing that Jim did for me right from the beginning was to help me recognize that I had an anger problem.

He has a very delicate personality and told me that the relationship could only work if he knew that he wasn't always going to feel like he was walking on eggshells with me. This was quite a revelation. No one had ever told me anything like that before, and I certainly never intended to make my partner feel uncomfortable with me in any way. It took me right back to my childhood, when I felt that same discomfort around my parents. I had a firm conviction never to let myself become like either of my parents, and here I was finding out that I had become just like both of them.

It was time to make some fundamental changes, not only in my behavior but also in the way that I looked at the world, and I knew that being around Jim's caring and gentle personality was what I needed to make these changes possible. He would spend the next several years helping me to see the error of my ways and helping me to recognize the distorted way that I was perceiving things that "happened to me" in life.

Whenever I would get really angry about a situation that occurred during my day, I would explain to Jim what had happened and he would go over it with me in detail. Often, he would then try to explain to me how my perception of the situation was incorrect, and would give me possible alternate ways of looking at it. These alternatives were always completely different than anything that would have occurred to me, and the insight helped me tremendously. I began to realize that everyone did not "have it in for me." I became aware that my anger was surfacing several times a day, and that I had developed a general dislike for people. I was regularly discovering new issues that stemmed from my anger.

My dislike for people was really a problem of tolerance and acceptance. I was constantly criticizing others' actions and words. Even watching a program on television was difficult because I would sit there and criticize peoples' clothes, hairstyle, words, speech patterns, situations . . . it went on and on. This was all brought to my attention when Jim revealed that he didn't enjoy watching television with me because the constant faultfinding made him uncomfortable, and his anxiety about the possibility of someone or something offending me overshadowed his ability to enjoy the show.

Another revelation came when Jim told me that he didn't want to play board games with me anymore.

Jim loves board games, and we would sometimes have family or friends over to play. During the games, I would get angry over small things that I perceived to be direct attacks on me as a person, but in reality were just part of normal game play.

Jim didn't like the way I was treating other players; it was ruining the experience for him, and he could no longer enjoy himself if I was a part of the game.

This was a harsh wake-up call for me. I loved Jim dearly and wanted us to share and participate in each other's hobbies and interests. It was hard to hear that he was unwilling to do this because of my personality. It was also frightening, because I didn't want to lose him.

I decided that this anger problem must come to an end, and I asked Jim to help me by pointing out when I was judging others harshly, or reacting in an angry manner to something that did not call for that kind of reaction.

After five years of marriage to Jim, I was finally able to say that I no longer had an anger problem. Jim agreed. Getting to that point was one of the most difficult things that I've ever done because it involved really changing my personality, and also changing the way that I thought about life.

Jim is the main inspiration for my growth during these years and I am so grateful that he was willing to help me. Finding a person who cared about me enough to help me with this long pain-staking process was all I ever wanted.

Along the way, I did use other tools to facilitate the process. I spent much time reading self-help books, for example, and meditating for additional direction. Just by listening to my inner voice every day really helped me to bring out the beauty that I was holding within.

Jim told me how proud he was that I had worked so hard to overcome my issues. He said that now I only got upset when the situation warranted it.

Life was so much better from this point on. I could honestly say for the first time that I liked who I was as a person. How I reacted to situations was so much different now than in any previous time of my life – I felt that I had grown tremendously. However, not everything in my life was going the way I wanted.

Things were still going wrong for me much of the time. When something went wrong, I now dealt with it as a "mature adult," that is, someone who just accepted that this was the way things were, and handled whatever the problem was, and moved on.

What I did not understand was that all the "wrong" things that were happening to me were happening because I still was not completely finished with my growth. I had changed my personality to become so much more of the person that I wanted to be, but my thoughts were still negative a good deal of the time. I still did not believe that I had control over the events and circumstances that came into my life. I would imagine negative outcomes for goals that I had. I was always waiting for the other shoe to drop when something good happened.

I didn't understand that my thoughts were affecting my life so much. I thought that if the words didn't come out of my mouth, then there was no harm being done. After all, no one else knew of these critical thoughts that I was thinking.

I was a very pleasant person to be around because I wanted to be viewed that way by others. But I still did not have the love for myself that was a necessary ingredient for eliminating the mental negativity that was preventing my life from unfolding the way I wanted it to.

It was not until 2006, upon seeing the movie "The Secret," that I finally had my breakthrough. It was such a powerful "Aha!" moment that I was in tears by the end of the film.

I had been in a women's group for about a year up to this point. Our monthly get-togethers were both meaningful and fun for me. The friend who hosted these meetings came up with the topic that we would cover each month, and it was always different, and always extremely interesting. In September, 2006, my friend told me that she had heard about "The Secret" and wanted that to be the topic for our next meeting. I had not heard of the movie, but I volunteered to obtain a copy of it to bring to the meeting.

Only three ladies were able to attend the women's group that evening, but I think it was a very profound experience for the three of us who were there; we each have had spectacular life journeys since that day.

I knew that after seeing it, "The Secret" was my missing link. I realized that even after listening to Esther Hicks all those years since my sister's death, I was still not practicing the Law of Attraction intentionally.

I was still thinking negatively, foreseeing negative outcomes to situations I was in and events that were happening in my life. This was another difficult realization for me, and I was quite hard on myself until I began to understand that my lack of self-love was the problem.

I was starting to realize the error of my ways. I knew that I was still critical in my thoughts, and negative in my general feelings much of the time. The happy face was there part of the time, the new me that had no anger, however I was still maintaining a façade when I wasn't feeling happy. I would just fake it in public when I wasn't feeling good, presenting my normal friendly self to others, because that's how I wanted to be seen.

I could honestly say that the anger was gone, but there remained a residual negativity that continued to affect the way I looked at the world. "The Secret" helped me to understand that I had one more major change to make. Somehow, I had to learn to stop the negative thinking. It was not apparent to me at the time that much of this negativity was derived from the way I felt about myself. Nevertheless, I was motivated to begin my new life of feeling good.

I started right away. I would watch the movie at least once a week, every Sunday. I wanted my work week to start off right, and knew that if I was feeling positive and motivated from watching the movie, I would do better. This worked well, and my life started changing. I started coming into money, for example, unexpectedly and regularly. Not just a few dollars, but thousands of dollars. In my career, the number of clients that were referred to me increased dramatically. My income was peaking and I was able to buy things that I had only dreamt of before. I decided to attract the money for a luxury hybrid car, and within a month I had the money to buy this car with cash.

My husband and I created "dream board" collages of pictures and phrases representing things that we wanted in life. Not just material things, but intangibles like happiness would be represented on the board as a simple phrase stating, "Be Happy!" Anything that we wanted to have happen for us would go on the dream board or be written in a list which I would review daily.

One by one, all of the things on both of our dream boards started happening for us. I was amazed at this change in our lives, and my husband said he had never seen me so happy. We were riding the wave of motivation and were on a high from all the great things that we were attracting to us.

Things were not perfect, though. There were still some very unfortunate things happening in my life, and I could not understand why. I realized later that many of the negative "thought seeds" that I had planted throughout my life were still sprouting;

growing beneath the surface and finally breaking through to manifest as negative events.

These events finally began to make sense to me. Something bad would happen, and I would go back in my memory, trying to locate the thought seed that was related to the event at hand, and I would always find the source. It invariably turned out to be some negative idea that I had believed to be true prior to my change. Because of my conviction about this idea at the time, and my subsequent failure to address and correct it, it was now coming to fruition.

I was still hard on myself because of this, and did not completely understand how all of this worked. I could feel good and think good thoughts, but when something went wrong, I blamed myself. By not loving myself completely, and not forgiving myself for any transgressions, I was making it impossible to experience my total growth potential.

At first, this was quite discouraging for me. I knew that I had been thinking negatively for so much of my life that it would be coming back to haunt me for years to come. It seemed inevitable. Then I realized that how I react to these events is completely up to me. How I think about these events can be changed.

This was a new "aha!" moment for me. Once I started to change my thoughts, and to really believe that good can come out of any situation, is when good started coming out of those situations. I was amazed to see how something that could be perceived as "bad" became something that, in the end, was a good experience because I decided to look at it differently and not punish myself for it mentally.

And I knew that there would be other people coming into my life who would not understand the Law of Attraction, and who would have negative things happen to them that might also affect me.

Again, I decided to look at these situations as opportunities for growth and try to see what good could come out of them instead of dwelling on the negative. Just by making this simple change, I can now honestly say that, in the end, everything goes right for me.

I have the ability to make my life magnificent every day and in every situation. It all comes down to my perceptions, thoughts, and feelings surrounding each event. All of these things are completely up to me at all times.

Sometimes this requires me to step back and look at the big picture. It takes trying to remove myself emotionally from what is happening. I can let myself feel negative, or I can try to think of something that makes me feel better. Making myself feel better is easy when I really want to – I just need to think of something that makes me happy on a consistent basis and immediately I start feeling better.

Chapter Nine

Your Relationship with Money

I shared my story with you to give you a window into my past – to help you see that no matter how bad things are, you can change your life and make it great. I wanted to share the techniques that worked so well in helping me to change my life, so that you can use them to change your own life. Decide how these techniques can best work for you, and make them your own. You can take all of the principles herein and apply them to any facet of your life.

One problem that I have had for most of my adult life, despite the fact that I was earning a six-figure income, was how I felt about money.

The relationship that I had with money as a young adult was like a tug-of-war. I had a mother who had taught me through her actions that money was something that was hard to come by, hard to keep, and when you didn't have it, life became very difficult.

After my parents divorced when I was five, my mother found herself with no real job skills (she did not finish college until much later in life). She worked very low-paying jobs and did not know how to manage the small amount of money that she brought in. We were evicted regularly for non-payment of rent, which resulted in my sister and I attending 18 different schools between kindergarten and ninth grade.

I learned from watching my mother's financial struggles, and knew that I did not want to be like her when it came to money. While I have learned from my mother's mistakes, I cannot say that she has made much progress with her relationship with money. My mother never was open to learning the principles that I explain in this book, and is still experiencing all the same money issues that have been plaguing her life for decades.

My father is an exact opposite creature from my mother when it comes to money. He was always obsessed with making money. Looking back, I'm convinced that money was my father's main love in life.

While growing up, I observed from him that every penny should be hoarded, even at the expense of those you love. He would only pay my mother a pittance for child support, $35/week in 1975, so that he could save his money. The poverty that I lived in as a child was very much due to the fact that my father paid nearly nothing for the support of my sister and me.

One summer, my grandmother gave money to my father to send me to tennis camp. He asked me if I wanted to go, but he didn't tell me that my grandmother was paying for it. Instead, he made up stories about how poor we were.

So when he asked if I wanted to go, I said "No, I know you can't afford it." He never said another word, and I never went to camp. He kept the money for himself! I learned the truth years later, when my grandmother said to me that she could never understand why I didn't want to go to tennis camp when she had given my father the money for it.

Growing up with two parents who had such dysfunctional views about money made it very difficult to avoid acquiring the same unhealthy attitudes. However, instead of accepting this legacy of greed, fear, and negativity surrounding money, I was determined to be different.

When I was sixteen, and becoming an independent young woman, I had resolved to show myself and the world that I could be good with money. I was trying to buck this training that I had grown up with.

I applied for a department store credit card and was approved. I then opened my own checking account.

With both of these tools, I began to build my credit and establish good spending habits. I used the credit card regularly and paid off the balance promptly each month.

It worked out wonderfully and I was soon on my way to becoming a responsible adult. When I turned eighteen, I applied for a Visa card to test my creditworthiness and found that I had done a good job – approved. Later that year, I bought a car and obtained a loan that did not require a co-signer.

I had a firm conviction about the importance of my monetary responsibilities. To this day, I have never paid a bill late, and I have perfect credit as a result.

These good habits and monetary responsibility will make life much easier when, for example, you need to convince a lender that you are good for the money. If you have not had success in keeping your bills under control and paying on time, keep reading – I'll help you to improve your relationship with money. By changing the way that you think about money, you can see miraculous turnarounds in a very short time.

I learned this lesson myself during my own journey to build a positive relationship with money. I would often find that after I paid all the bills, there was no money left. I was living paycheck to paycheck, continually paying off one debt just to have another arise. Why was this happening? Why couldn't I get ahead? The answer lay in the fact that one simple word was missing from my vocabulary. Abundance. I didn't know that it existed.

If you look at your life, how many times have you gone without a meal to feed yourself and those that you care for? I asked myself this question and realized that even when times were tight growing up, we never starved. There was always something to eat, no matter how sparse. If we ran out of food, others would come and bring bags of food over to help our family get by. Even though we moved from place to place because of eviction, we always had a place to sleep every night with a roof over our heads. At the very lowest points in my life, there was always enough to get by.

When you look at the concept of abundance, that is what it is really showing us. No matter how bad things have been, abundance remains and makes sure that all are cared for. During my life, I grew to learn that no matter how bad it was, things would always be okay. This gave me a sense of comfort and was the basis that I grew to believe in abundance. Believing that there is great abundance has been a great attractor for me to an abundant life.

While I believed in abundance as a fundamental truth about always having enough, I still was not able to get ahead regardless of how much money I was making. My inability to save money was being caused by my own negative thoughts and feelings. I believed that abundance was there to make sure that I always had enough to get by so that I would not go without. I was holding myself back with this limiting thought. This thought was limiting because I stopped at the point of having enough to get by, but never going further to allowing myself to want and have the extra things in life. Abundance is there so that there is more than enough of everything in this world for all to have, without worry.

If you pay your bills on time every month, yet are not happy about the amount of money coming in or the amount left over, then you are already halfway to your goal of making more money!

If you don't pay all your bills due to lack of funds, then you are starting your journey now to having a better relationship with money.

All you need to do is put your mind and mood in a happier state when you have any thoughts about money. Think of having true abundance for yourself. As soon as anything having to do with money enters into your head, make sure that the thoughts are positive – not negative.

If you ever have the following types of situations happen to you, then you are perpetuating a struggle with money:

Go shopping and look at the price tag on an item and think, "I can't afford that."

Get a bill in the mail and become sad, angry, depressed or any other bad feeling.

See someone else who needs money and think," I don't have enough to help that person and pay my own bills."

Cry over not having enough money.

Call a creditor on the phone or go in person to that place of business and then argue with the service person about the bill.

Feel jealous of someone who has more money than you.

Argue with your spouse over money.

Tell your kids, "I don't have the money for that right now."

Each of these actions negates your ability to draw money to yourself. They are big, bold statements to yourself reinforcing the negative idea that you do not have enough money. No matter what it takes to re-train your brain, you need stop thinking this way if you want more money to come to you!

If you have a hard time talking about money without going in a negative direction, then don't talk about it unless you can first put yourself into a positive mental and emotional state. This will help to combat that tendency toward negativity.

Listen to your words as you talk to others. You may sometimes catch yourself saying things that reflect a "lack mentality." Even when listening to another person talk about her problems, it's natural to agree for the sake of being agreeable, saying things like, "yeah, I know it must be rough."

Instead, you could be offering an uplifting thought or changing the subject if you can't come up with a way to make things sound more positive. I talk with a lot of people every day about their money, and sometimes, they just have their minds made up as to how bad they've got it. It seems to happen the most when I am talking with someone who does not know about how to attract good things into their life.

It can be a bit of a trap at first when these situations arise, since you don't want to be rude and tell the person to stop talking like that. You also don't want to walk away and end the conversation abruptly. It takes a great deal of self-discipline to counteract another person's negativity in a constructive manner.

So for example, if you are shopping with someone and they look at an expensive item and shriek, "Would you look at the price of this? I could never afford that!" Then a positive and simple statement that would help to turn around the negative energy could be, "You know, if you decide you really want it, you could find a way to afford it." Or "I know you, and I've seen you when you really want something – you make it happen for yourself!"

Uttering a simple and uplifting sentence can do two things: first, it can help to keep your energy positive (very important), and second, it may spark an important change of thought in the other person. Trying to go any further with your statements is not necessary, unless the other person really is interested and prompts you for more.

If she comes back with probing questions, that is a good sign and you can give some examples of how this new way of thinking has worked for you.

If, however, she comes back with an unintentionally defensive statement, then it is clear that she is not ready to hear this information. Not everyone you come across will get these concepts right away. Some will never grasp them or agree with them. It is important that you accept others' personal choices, because in doing so, you are offering the same degree of freedom that you want for yourself. Remember that each person begins this life with their own learning curve, so give them room to grow at their own speed. To explain this statement further, if you look at two five year old girls who were born on the same day, one may be more mature while the other more intelligent. These are two human components that each of us lives with every day, yet the pace of learning relating to both topics will always be different for each person.

When dealing with someone who is not at the same point that you are regarding a specific topic, don't make it uncomfortable for them by arguing your point. Instead, move the conversation to a different, more neutral topic as soon as possible.

You will get better at counteracting others' negativity as time goes on, but just remember that it is easy to get sucked into their crying game if you aren't careful. This is where living in the present really helps. By giving your full attention to the current situation, you will be able avoid the pitfalls quickly and easily.

One little trick that really works is "intending." Intend for harmony and happy situations as you enter into different segments of your day. Just say to yourself, "As I go into this store, I will think and feel abundantly. Everything that I need will be completely affordable and I will leave here with a feeling of fulfillment and gratefulness."

If you recite a deliberate set of intentions to yourself before every undertaking, you can arrive at the best possible outcome every single time. Try it!

I would like to help re-train your thoughts about money by having you think about a time when you had a bad feeling associated with something money-related. While I don't want to bring up those bad feelings again, I do want your memory of events to help you discover bad habits so that you can change them.

So, when did this negative association with money occur? Was it when you found out that something you purchase regularly just went up in price?

Was it when you did your bills?

Was it when you looked in your wallet and saw no money?

Was it when you looked at your bank account balance?

Was it when you talked with your spouse about money?

Bringing these situations into the forefront will help you to think about any recurring themes that come up for you. These recurring trends need to be changed right away.

If you said that one of those times was related to your bills, let's set some parameters that may help you.

Never look at your mail while in a bad mood. Always put a smile on your face before you even pick it up. If you can't think of anything to make you smile, then wait until you can.

Open all the envelopes face-down and all at once. This way you don't have any thoughts about who they are from. Once they're all opened, keeping your smile, begin to remove the items and sort them.

Bills go into one pile. Don't look at the bill amount unless you can do so and still remain happy. All the other mail, sort as necessary. If you find things that are non-bills that you like to look at more while you're opening, spend as much time as you'd like on these items.

Once you've sorted all the mail and decided what is trash and what are keepers, put the bills in a "to be paid" designated place. If you generally know when all of your bills are due, the best policy is to pick a day sometime before the earliest due date and just pay them all at once. Now you are really only thinking about the bills once or twice a month. If you can, set up auto-payment plans or use your bank's online bill payment service to facilitate getting this task completed as quickly as possible each month. If you don't look at the amounts, because they are automatically paid, there is less opportunity for you to think about your bills and dwell on them. This simplifies your life and also ensures that the bills are paid on time. Another good idea is to make sure that you have overdraft protection in place on your checking account. This way you won't have to worry if you come up short one month.

Doing these things will help to keep you in a good mood instead of having a sinking feeling in your stomach every time you open the mail or take time to pay bills.

If you don't feel that you are ready to follow these suggestions and still feel positive, then ask someone else in your household to open the mail or pay bills for you if possible. Find someone who is able to do the task without attaching emotion to it.

When I first started following this method, I did find it easier to let my husband open the mail and pay the bills because I was so affected emotionally. It helped tremendously that I didn't look at the total amount that was coming out of our account every month.

This was the way that we did it for about a year, until I had adjusted my thought processes to the point where I could start feeling good about paying the bills. Yes, that's right – feeling GOOD about paying the bills. I just decided to look at it differently when I started paying the bills myself again.

I was thankful that we always had enough income to pay all the bills. I told myself to think of abundance. We have never been on the street without a place to live, we have never paid a bill late, and we have not missed any meals. We have had our family vacations every year because there has always been enough.

At one point where I was changing jobs and had to wait a few months to receive income, I was robbing Peter to pay Paul (taking a cash advance out on my credit card to cover all the bills). I considered it a wonderful thing that we even had this option available to us so that we were not late on any bills. I still told myself that we were doing great, and the fact that we had everything that we NEEDED in life is what put me in a better frame of mind. When paying bills online, I would enter each amount and say to myself, "Yeah, I have enough money to pay that!" and then smile to myself.

Once all the bills were paid, I knew that I was finished for the whole month, and that put me in a great mood.

Something amazing happened within a year of doing this. There really was enough money to pay all the bills every month. The lesser-paying job that I had taken after moving led to a promotion to a job that paid three times as much money, and I truly did have enough to cover all the bills that I had built up during the troubled times.

Again you can see that no matter how deeply in debt you are or how desperate your money situation seems – it can get better with just a simple change in your thoughts and habits. Stop thinking about how bad it is, and do whatever it takes to focus on the fortunate things happening in your life.

Once you are able to achieve this mental paradigm shift, you can then start setting your sights on bigger and better goals relating to money.

When you are ready, you can design any monetary goal that you can dream and put it into your top 5 list. If you love you and know that you deserve this in your life, it will happen for you very quickly.

I did this myself and went from earning $60,000 to $150,000 in one year. I simply accepted that I had real value and worth, and that I'm very good at what I do for a living. I did not embark on any get-rich-quick ventures, nor did I change my career.

I was aware that there were people out there at various levels in my industry who were making much more than me, and I knew in my mind and heart that they were no better and no worse than me. This put me on a level playing field with them, and made it very easy for me to see myself making much more money in my field.

So after reaching the goal of making $150,000 a year, I decided to set my sights higher. The very next year, as a New Year's resolution, I made a new goal for my income. I wanted to be making $300,000; I wanted it to happen by the end of the year, and I wanted the job to find me. I did not want to have to look for the job. Ten months later, in October, I learned that one of my associates was retiring. She had been in her position for sixteen years, and upper management was giving her the option of choosing her replacement. Knowing that I was a caring person, and good at what I do, she approached me and asked if I would be willing to take over her job. She needed my decision by December.

I had a lot to think about since the job, while with the same company, was in another state. I realized that I had not been specific enough in my original intent to obtain a $300,000-per-year job. I said that I wanted one, but I did not say where. I did decide by December that I would take the job. It was, after all, an offer of a lifetime.

I got choked up as I thought about how this opportunity came to me in exactly the way that I had said that I wanted it to. I finally "got it" – this wasn't just some fanciful belief. Things were really happening for me exactly the way that I intended for them to happen. I realized that this is all up to me and that I can set any goal that I want and achieve it.

The same is true for you. It is true for any person that wants to make it true. Take however many steps you need to get to your monetary goals. Sometimes you need to start small and work very slowly with lots of positive reinforcement to see that it works.

If you believe in your dreams and truly wish to see them realized, they will happen for you.

Chapter Ten

Accepting Others into Your Life

We have been talking a lot about you and me. If life were just about one or two people, then it would be so much easier working these concepts without interruption or distraction.

The truth is that all of the people that we encounter have a profound effect on who we are as human beings. We allow it to be this way. Our society has trained us to care very much about what others think and how they act toward us.

If the cashier who is checking you out in line at the grocery store has a rude attitude and is less than pleasant to deal with, you are taught to question it. When questioning it, self-blame can be one reaction. "What did I do to make her treat me this way?"

Another reaction might be to give the same treatment right back. Or just the opposite, you may try to cheer her up by saying something nice.

Whatever the reaction, at its core is the fact that you care about what they think of you, and so you are responding in the way that you have been trained is appropriate.

I ask you to think about it in a different way. Is that person really someone that you want to give any of your energy to? If you are spending any amount of time after such an interaction trying to figure out why the person was acting a certain way, you are effectively giving your energy away. You are diminishing your personal empowerment. This is precious time and energy that you could have used nurturing happiness and feeling joy. Any amount of time that you take away from being happy and joyful is only serving to lengthen the pathway to your goals.

It is just not worth it to give that type of energy to others. Especially not to people with whom you have no relationship to consider. It is best to just allow them to be in their bad mood, try to distance yourself as much as possible from any interaction, and then move on as quickly as possible.

Repeating a simple mantra at these times can help to remind you that dwelling on it is not worth the time or energy. Say something like, "I want to see only that which I want to see."

As you say this, visualize a picture of the person's face in your mind. Take your hand and grab that visual picture and throw it in an imaginary trash can. It creates a sense of closure to the problem and makes you feel better that you have thrown this problem away and have decided not to spend any more of your precious time or energy on it.

That is the first way that you can allow others to be who they are and for you to be who you are. It works in perfect sync. You leave them to be the unpleasant people that they are choosing to be, and you move on to continue having your good day. Accept that they have made this choice for themselves and allow them to be in the space that they want to be in.

Acceptance is easy enough to achieve with strangers, casual acquaintances, and people that you deal with on an occasional basis. It is much harder with people you care about, have a relationship with, and want to spend time with.

While you are more emotionally attached to the latter, you can still practice this application in short term situations and see if it helps you to find some relief. If you do find relief for a short period with this technique, then you might find that your relationship starts to change.

Let's say that you have a spouse who does not help out with all of the things that you would like him to do around the house. Cooking, laundry, vacuuming, washing dishes, general cleaning, deep cleaning all need to be done on a periodic basis and you don't know that his help is a small percentage of getting these tasks done. You are taking on a much heavier load and don't think it is fair to have to do so much more. This is a common problem that exists in many households today and creates a great deal of strife. There are many positive avenues to solving this predicament, it really is up to you to think of what positive solution exists that best coincides with your desires.

The first step towards this positive solution is to accept the other person for who he is. If you want to continue your relationship with this person and he means a great deal to you in your life, then acceptance of who he is will be the first step towards harmony. This does not mean that you will not continue to work on your issue of having to complete a great deal of house work, it means that you are going to accept that in the length of time that you have had a relationship with this person, you now know him well enough to know that he will not uphold completing what you consider to be a proportionate percentage of house work.

Once you have come to this acceptance, you have now made the decision to approach this issue from a place of acceptance and harmony. It will make future talks about this subject proceed in a much smoother fashion.

Next, create an intention that you would like to find the solution on getting your house work completed up to your standards, and you want to find the people who are willing to perform those jobs consistently. Let the answers flow to you. You may find that talking with your husband about which tasks he would like to do will also help to reveal which tasks he does not like to do. If you find that neither of you enjoy performing a certain household task, is it possible that another person could do this task? Try to negotiate openly and evenly with all of the people in your household that are impacting these tasks.

The biggest factor that will determine success here is how much you really have begun to allow the other person(s) to be who they are without judgment, and without trying to change them.

Trying to change someone to fit into the mold that you want them in is the very activity that you are trying to avoid from others. You want the freedom to make your own choices for yourself with your own true thoughts and feelings. Give the other person the space to do the same.

You can't change the world; you can only change yourself and how you react to the world. Why not be a happier person and just accept the world and the people in it, and accept the situations that they have brought into their lives as a result of their own free decisions? This will lead to less self-judgment, and more self-loving. You will feel more acceptance of yourself, and more comfort doing what you think you should be doing with your own life. It has to start somewhere. Try allowing yourself to be who you are first by following the beginning sections of this book. Remember that you are finding the real you who loves and cares about you. Find out what is important to you and allow yourself to fulfill your dreams. Then allow others to be who they are, and you will have gained true freedom of self. No more judging others, no more judging you.

You have seen what stages I went through in my own life to get to where I am today. I have shared with you some of my personal experiences to help you appreciate the fact that no matter what point you have come to right now – no matter what brought you here – you are able to recalibrate yourself and your life. You are able to make it the right life for you. That is one of the most liberating feelings that there is. With this knowledge you can go anywhere you want to. You can change your geographic location temporarily or permanently. You can introduce new hobbies, habits, and ways of living into each and every day. You can choose to meet new people, or enhance the relationships with the people that are part of your life now.

That is really where I'm going with this. You have the ability to surround yourself with whom you want and have them be part of your life experience. If you decide that there are those who make you feel less than good when you are with them, there are a couple of courses of action you can take. Actually, there are many ways to do this; the possibilities are infinite. However, I have a couple to prime the pump.

If you have someone in your life whom you care dearly about, but who has behavioral traits that do not make you feel good – take the focus off of those things when you are with that person. Start bringing up new topics of conversation that you have not brought up before. Think about what topics you can discuss that are positive and that you have a mutual interest in. Bring these various topics up with him and see where it takes you.

It can help to make a list of the things that you like about this person, even if you can only think of one or two. When you see him, really focus on those items. Give him compliments relating to the things that you like about him. See how it changes the conversation.

Trying to remove negativity can be hard unless you really focus on the positive here. If you practice saying to him repeatedly in your head, "I love you," you will find it increasingly difficult to feel any negativity.

Before starting a conversation, remember to develop a specific intent of how you want the conversation to go. Do you want to find humor? Do you want to have a happy discussion? Do you enjoy a good banter back and forth – an exchange of differing opinions? What is it that you would like to create in the conversation that will make you feel good? Now visualize it and create the scene in your mind. Imagine how you want it to go. Start out by saying, "I want to have a great conversation that makes me happy and leaves me feeling fulfilled."

During this brief precursor to the conversation, avoid thinking about any problems you've had with this person in the past. If negative thoughts arise, or you find yourself engaging in a mental argument with the person, then end the scene immediately. Get back to a mentally and emotionally balanced state of mind before trying again. Remember, how the conversation develops is up to you; it depends upon being proactive before the conversation begins, and upon how you react to the other person during the conversation.

One of the most important things that I learned many years ago is that I don't need to be right. I don't need to be right. If I find that I am becoming perturbed by someone's condescending tone and know-it-all attitude, I just say to myself, "I don't need to be right." I have taken my pride out of it, allowing her to be in her space without me needing to try to gain the upper hand. After all, what does it matter if I gain the upper hand? Trying to get there will make me feel worse than if I just let it go and tell myself that I don't need to be right.

If you keep coming to a negative place in your visualizations, stop and try to evaluate the way that you feel. Why are you feeling this way? Why do you keep coming to a negative place in your mind, when the purpose of these role-playing scenes is to help you have a better relationship with this person. Are you ready to have a positive relationship with him? Is it possible that it could be you who has the underlying problem while you have been blaming the other person all along?

Stop and look at yourself when you find that you are placing blame on another person, and ask what it is that you could be doing to allow a conflict to exist. If you look at this openly and find that you are indeed contributing to the conflict, then it's time to delve into the nucleus of your issue. What is the hump that you can't get over here? Is it pride? Anger? Resentment? Jealousy? Frustration? Lack of ability to communicate your true feelings?

I'm throwing out a lot of possibilities here, and it may be that some or none of these reasons apply to you. Only you know the answer. It is inside of you.

Remember, it takes two to tango, and if you choose not to dance, then no one is doing the tango.

It is best to do your problem-solving when you are in a good place mentally. If the solution isn't apparent to you during a conflict, then distance yourself from it as quickly as possible. See what you can bring to the table when you are happier and more objective.

After trying this for a while, go back to those mental conversations that went awry and see if they now start to go in a more positive direction. You may find that you are now more easily able to produce happy thoughts when you think about the other person.

When you revisit real-life conversations you've had that resulted in conflict, concentrate on the things that you said that may have fueled the conflict, and change those things in your mind by saying something less contentious in their place. This is another technique that can you can use to create closure more quickly.

Bringing up the issue again with him would only be risking another bad experience. Dwelling on what was said will only serve to keep recreating this bad experience for you, bringing you more unhappiness.

This is the way to unburden yourself from the past, and let it go much more quickly. Change an unpleasant conversation into a pleasant one by going over it in your mind and changing what you've said. Now you can feel better about the whole thing and you can move on.

Accepting others for who they are without the goal of changing them or judging them for their words or actions can be one of the great challenges inside yourself. And yes, it is inside you where the challenge lies.

One thing that I'll bring up again is the importance of getting yourself to feel joy, be happy, and to eliminate the negative mind-chatter that you have been conditioned to generate for much of your life. You need to get yourself to that happy point, and accept the fact that other humans are going to be a part of your life. They are going to continue to exist here with you for the duration of your existence on this earth. The faces may change, but your ability to deal with all the faces you come into contact with will stay the same.

If you really want a specific person in your life, and you want to feel good when you are around him – then it is time to make that list of things you really like or love about him.

Do this with each person who is important to you, with whom you have issues. Even if you can't seem to get past what someone does that makes you crazy you can always go back to this list in your mind. You'll remember what you do like, and smile.

Chapter Eleven

Bringing it All Together

From a "big picture" point of view, can you conceptualize yourself accepting and rejoicing in the diversity of the human race? That sounds like an idealistic point of view, however if you hold any beliefs at all about having a purpose on this planet that includes being here to experience, grow, love and live life to the fullest while having a joyful existence, then embrace what this means for you.

The more you push against others for being who they are, the more you push away the joy that can be yours all of the time.

If you spend a great deal of your time judging and criticizing others, whether vocally or in the privacy of your thoughts, what you are really doing is pressing the pause button on your own joy and happiness. You are pausing so that you can take the time to squeeze in this powerful negativity.

You may think that somehow you are helping people by identifying flaws in them. You may feel superior, sitting in judgment and assessing their errors and shortcomings. You may feel sympathy for them. You may feel disgust. Whatever you are feeling that is associated with a criticism is going to bring you down. There is nothing positive to be gained in pulling someone else down.

If you want to help others with their lives, be happy with yourself. They will naturally try to be more like you because you have the ability to be happy.

If you are bringing them down with your opinions and critiques – how are they going to feel each time they see you? Unworthy? Bitter? Resentful?

Instead, bring your best self to the dance and see how others join in. Your success is evident when others try to emulate you. In like manner, you can feel free to emulate the person(s) whom you admire most. It can be a daisy chain of great inspiration, one person to the next.

There is one important point that I want to bring you back to here – always be who you want you to be, not what you think others want you to be. The whole reason that a person will come to admire you is because you are an original, not an actor.

You can look at what other people do in life, internalize it, make it right for you, and then incorporate those traits into your own way of living.

That is not mimicking – it is seeing something in another person that you would like to express in yourself, as a part of who you are. When you do this, visualize yourself being this way, not the person whom you saw and admired. This is really how you make it your own. You see yourself in this light.

So we have come full circle in our exploration of your relationships with others. Much of the game is how you are playing it. How seriously are you taking the game? If you find that you are taking it too seriously, letting every little thing that others do affect you dramatically, dwelling on things for hours, days, weeks, months, or years – all of this wasted time is preventing you from living in the moment.

Living in the moment keeps you in touch with your feelings, allows you to give due attention to present events, gives you more control over the course of those events, and keeps you from dwelling on the past. The past is only as alive as you let it be. If you keep reliving unpleasant scenes from the past, how is that going to make you feel better? How is that going to help you grow?

Is living in the past keeping you from fulfilling all the hopes and dreams that you have for yourself today? Is it helping to recreate the same bad situations over and over?

Stop this cycle. Know where your weak link is. Be willing to identify it and then find your solutions. I say solutions because there are many ways to get yourself into a better mood and ultimately a better life. Feel happy by whatever means you can.

So a new list that you need to make for yourself is how to make yourself happy and bring joy into your life.

As you come across someone who is having a bad day, refer to your list and come to an understanding with yourself that this is not going to upset your balance and change the course of your day or your life. You will acknowledge that this person has no power over you or your life and that you choose to be happy even if he or she is not. They may be in the same bad place that you were at one point and the best thing that they could use right now is an understanding and positive word or two.

As you grow, you will find that you have a deep love for yourself. This love will expand to include love for others. As a person does something to upset you, visualizing the person and creating feelings of love within will diffuse your anger, and keep you in a positive frame of mind.

Choose joy. Allow others to choose their own experience. Experience your life in exactly the way that you intend it for yourself.

Now practice, practice, practice these techniques. Remind yourself that your resolution to succeed is your top priority. Keep your top-five list focused in your mind daily. Make time for you to do this.

Your new attitude and intent will infuse positive energy into your everyday activities, and will become a part of your daily planning, and you will begin to have more and more positive experiences as a result. These experiences, flowing one into the other, will make for a happy, wonderful, magical life. This knowledge will develop into inner wisdom as you live these experiences. The magic is yours and is in you every moment that you choose to have it there. Now go create the experiences that you want to have a fulfilling life!

Manufactured by Amazon.ca
Bolton, ON

18818664R00062